First Published by Ink Gladiators Press®

Translations Of Hope

Editor-in-Chief: Reena Doss

First Edition
ISBN 13: 978-93-49117-42-6

High Standards For You - Lantern 7

Credits:
Book Design by Leonie Belle Hawk
Hindi & Chinese (Simplified) Translations: Edited and Proofed by Justin Adam Wolf and Aelius Arche

Ink Gladiators Press®
Publishing and promoting warriors on life's battlefield
Founded in 2019 | Bangalore, India
www.inkgladiatorspress.com

To my beloved Weaver,

Thank you for the privilege of living
in this beautiful world that holds so much wonder,
it always makes my heart ache whenever I see, feel and sense
your love in everything that you create for us to enjoy

To my future family,

I hope you always appreciate, care and stand up for
every living being that walks on the land,
swims in the waters, and flies in the skies

To my dear Epigrammatists,

may we remember the impact of a feeling,
a thought, a reflection when we write which may read
as a statement or a micro poem or loose idea,
but is in fact, the wisdom of a quote

This book is a lantern of

High Standards For You

Love Adores
Never-ending Tales:
Eagerly Ready, News Sails

These quotes are full of my favourite animals, birds and ocean creatures or those mammals that love the water. Originally written in English, these poetic quotes have been translated into Hindi and Chinese (Simplified).

High Standards For You

Because Mental Health Matters

I stopped numbering my pages because my story is still being written.

Besides, I do like its symbol a lot—a sleeping 8.

I'll find you in the dark because I'm the girl

who loves to stay *lost* amongst the midnight stars

caught up with moonbeams *in a lantern*

trying to find my way back *home*

LANTERNS

The pleasure of watching light move across the night sky against its deep purples, blues and greys is an incredible sight to behold.

Though I have never seen it in person myself except on TV, reels or videos, I would imagine that it mimics the feeling of a thousand golden suns glimmering brighter than the stars behind them. I would imagine that it would capture the feeling of remembering that we are each important because no matter how small or big we are light travels faster than sound. I would imagine it would make anyone who sees them smile, open their hearts as hope flutters like birdsong near their door, and the taste of something indescribably good wraps them warmly.

Lanterns are necessary because igniting hope is the best cure in support of mental health awareness. Many live in darkness, in a state of feeling disillusioned by those they put their faith in and have forgotten how to see their own hearts through eyes that love, but a lantern is meant for just this purpose—to relight someone's candle with kindness, to hold a hand steadily in their shadows, and to listen gently to the broken pieces in others speaking. Sometimes, the truth is simple.

That delicate point between human nature and the desire to do what is good is where we will meet the Author of Love. Love can only be known from the One who created us and even when people (who follow God) make us feel like He isn't real or there for us, one of the best ways to reconnect with Him directly is to love with all your heart—and to balance it with healthy discernment, boundaries and truth in situations where your broken parts might want to do, feel or say the exact opposite. *E.g.: Jesus Christ*

It is my joy to let go of this lantern—as all lanterns must be—for others to find because I want to share something beautiful that I gained and that is mine to offer: You are deeply loved by Heavenly Hands that have constructed, created and command time, space, and distance.

Love holds the might, roar, and bravery
of a LION and a LAMB that stitches homes together
like a WEAVERBIRD to SEAL every corner
of the roof above because when the rain comes,
you'd be safe, cozy, and warm.

प्यार में एक शेर की ताकत, दहाड़ और बहादुरी होती है, जो एक वीवरबर्ड की तरह घरों को सिलता है, ताकि ऊपर की छत का हर कोना सील हो जाए, क्योंकि जब बारिश आती है, तो तुम सुरक्षित, आरामदायक और गर्म रहो।

High Standards For You

爱蕴藏着雄狮的威猛、咆哮与勇气

它如织布鸟般缝合家园

将屋顶的每个角落

牢牢封存

只因当风雨来袭

你将安然无恙，温暖如春

Reena Doss

Empathy is in the penetrating gaze
of a HORSE that looks deeply into your soul,
opens the big eyes of an OWL that stays awake
to listen to every story you want to share,
and in the company of an OTTER
that holds your hand to teach you
how to just float, let things go, and be.

सहानुभूति एक घोड़े की पैनी निगाहों में है जो आपकी आत्मा में गहराई से झाँकता है, एक उल्लू की बड़ी आँखें खोलता है जो आपकी हर कहानी सुनने के लिए जागता रहता है जिसे आप साझा करना चाहते हैं, और एक ऊदबिलाव की संगति में जो आपका हाथ पकड़कर आपको सिखाता है कि कैसे बस तैरना है, चीजों को जाने देना है, और बस होना है।

同理心藏在马儿
深邃凝视的眼神里，
如猫头鹰睁大的眼眸彻夜守候，
倾听你倾诉的每个故事，
更在水獭相伴时
牵起你的手教你
如何随波漂浮，放下一切，安然存在。

∞

Kindness moves in the soft paw
of your DOG taking care
to make you remember why you exist,
in the tunes of a NIGHTINGALE
that won't stop singing outside your window
and in the sweetest sounds of a WHALE
flipping and spouting water to remind
your heart of its capacity to expand.

दया आपके कुत्ते के नरम पंजे में चलती है, जो आपको यह याद दिलाने का ख्याल रखता है कि आप क्यों मौजूद हैं, एक कोयल की धुनों में, जो आपकी खिड़की के बाहर गाना बंद नहीं करती, और एक व्हेल की सबसे मीठी आवाज़ों में, जो आपके दिल को उसकी विस्तार करने की क्षमता की याद दिलाने के लिए पानी में उछलती और पानी का फव्वारा छोड़ती है।

∞

High Standards For You

善意栖息于爱犬轻柔的爪尖
它悉心照料着你
让你铭记存在的意义
流淌在夜莺窗外的歌声里
那旋律永不停歇
更在鲸鱼翻腾喷水的欢快声中
提醒你心胸的无限广阔

Reena Doss

The clever hunting game of a pod
of ORCAs invites **Respect**,
just like the screeching SEAGULL
that takes off into skies of freedom
and in the way your CAT decides
he needs to lean into your space,
when just moments before...
he couldn't be bothered if he annoyed you
for pushing things off your desk.

∞

ओर्का के झुंड का चतुर शिकार खेल सम्मान को आमंत्रित करता है, ठीक वैसे ही जैसे चिल्लाती हुई समुद्री बगुली जो स्वतंत्रता के आकाश में उड़ान भरती है, और जिस तरह आपकी बिल्ली तय करती है कि उसे आपके करीब आना है, जबकि कुछ ही पल पहले... उसे इस बात की कोई परवाह नहीं थी कि वह आपकी मेज से चीजें गिराकर आपको परेशान करती है।

虎鲸群聪慧的狩猎游戏
唤起敬畏之心，
正如鸣叫的海鸥
展翅飞向自由的天空，
更在爱猫决定
踱入你身侧的姿态里——
就在片刻之前…
它还毫不在意是否惹恼你
将桌物推落一地。

Humanity is in in the tusk
of an ELEPHANT that senses intention,
in the gentleness it exhibits
despite its core memories,
unlike a PARROT
who sometimes repeats itself,
not always because it forgets
but because it can't stop being obsessive
about what it loves the most,
and in the playfulness of a DOLPHIN
that knows exactly where its priorities lie.

मानवता एक हाथी के सूंड में है जो इरादे को भांपता है, उस कोमलता में जो वह अपनी गहरी यादों के बावजूद दिखाता है, एक तोते के विपरीत जो कभी-कभी खुद को दोहराता है, हमेशा इसलिए नहीं कि वह भूल जाता है, बल्कि इसलिए कि वह उस चीज़ के प्रति जुनूनी होना बंद नहीं कर सकता जिसे वह सबसे ज्यादा प्यार करता है, और एक डॉल्फिन की चंचलता में जो ठीक-ठीक जानती है कि उसकी प्राथमिकताएँ कहाँ हैं।

∞

人性存在于象牙之中
那象群感知意图的象牙
存在于它们展现的温柔里
纵然背负核心记忆
不同于鹦鹉
时而重复自身
并非因遗忘
而是无法停止痴迷
于最爱的存在
更存在于海豚的嬉戏间
它们深知何为优先之事

Faith is born in every LAMB
that knows its breath began within
the womb, or after the seed dies,
in the EAGLE that spreads its wings
like an anthem of the law that binds us,
even when we cannot see its loyalty
to the one who designed it to perfection,
and in the STARFISH we discover
on the beaches of our adventures
that reveal even they too
can fall from the sky.

विश्वास हर मेमने में जन्म लेता है जो जानता है कि उसकी साँस गर्भ में ही शुरू हुई थी, या बीज के मरने के बाद, उस गरुड़ में जो अपने पंखों को उस कानून के गान की तरह फैलाता है जो हमें बाँधता है, भले ही हम उस पर उसकी वफादारी न देख सकें जिसने उसे पूर्णता के साथ रचा था, और हमारे साहसिक तटों पर मिली तारामछली में हम यह पाते हैं कि वे भी आकाश से गिर सकती हैं।

信仰诞生于每只羔羊
它知晓自己的气息始于
母腹，或种子凋零之后
诞生于展翅的雄鹰
那羽翼如律法的颂歌将我们缚住
纵使我们看不见它对造物主的忠诚
那造物主将它雕琢得完美无瑕
诞生于海星
我们在冒险的海滩上发现它们
它们昭示着连它们自己
也可能从天而降

∞

Patience is in the cunning of a FOX that hides
and stealthily gathers what it needs to survive,
in the speed of a HUMMINGBIRD's wings
as it keeps itself adrift in mid-air
to appreciate the colours of a flower
and in the engrossed attention of a PENGUIN
in his dreamy choice to find the perfect pebble.

धैर्य, एक लोमड़ी की चालाकी में है जो छिपती है और चुपके से अपनी ज़रूरत की चीज़ें इकट्ठा करती है, एक हमिंगबर्ड के पंखों की तेज़ी में है जो हवा में तैरते हुए एक फूल के रंगों की सराहना करती है, और एक पेंगुइन के एकाग्र ध्यान में है जो अपने सपनों के पत्थर को खोजने के लिए एक आदर्श कंकड़ चुनता है।

High Standards For You

耐心藏于狐狸的狡黠
它隐匿身形悄然觅食维生
藏于蜂鸟振翅的迅疾
悬停空中细品花色
藏于企鹅专注的凝神
在寻觅完美鹅卵石的梦幻抉择中

Reena Doss

Integrity walks before and after
a PANTHER leaves his prints behind
to mark the reality of what lay
before buildings took his path,
in the dazzling display of a PEACOCK
as he does his best to showcase his worth
in the beauty of his feathers that he grew,
and in the unparalleled rarity of a pearl that grew
in the chaos of an OYSTER.

अखंडता एक तेंदुए के पदचिन्हों से पहले और बाद में चलती है, जो अपने पीछे निशान छोड़ता है, यह चिह्नित करने के लिए कि इमारतों के रास्ता काटने से पहले वहाँ क्या था, एक मोर के चकाचौंध प्रदर्शन में, जब वह अपने पंखों की सुंदरता के माध्यम से अपनी कीमत दिखाने की पूरी कोशिश करता है, जो उसने उगाए हैं, और एक सीप के कोलाहल में पले-बढ़े मोती की बेजोड़ दुर्लभता में।

正直如影随形
在黑豹留下足迹前后
标记着建筑物占据其路径前
曾存在的真实
在孔雀炫目的展示中
它竭力彰显自身价值
通过羽翼生成的美丽
以及珍珠无与伦比的珍稀
在牡蛎的混沌中孕育而成。

∞

Values exist in the quills of a PORCUPINE
that lift, rattle, and embed themselves
into mirrors that step on their right to just be.
They circle around in a ROBIN's breast
as he moves with seasons to align all that he feels,
just like a CRAB that upholds its courage
and persists on being known by the way
it sees, moves, and clings tenaciously to them.

मूल्य काँटेदार सूअर की कलमों में होते हैं जो उठते, खड़खड़ाते और खुद को ठूँस देते हैं उन दर्पणों में जो उनके बस होने के अधिकार पर पैर रखते हैं। वे एक गौरैया की छाती में घूमते हैं जब वह अपने एहसासों को मौसम के साथ मिलाने के लिए चलती है, ठीक वैसे ही जैसे एक केकड़ा अपनी हिम्मत बनाए रखता है और अपनी पहचान इस तरह बनाए रखने पर अड़ा रहता है जिस तरह वह देखता है, चलता है, और उन पर डटकर चिपका रहता है।

∞

刺猬的棘刺间藏着价值
它们竖起、震颤、扎入
那些践踏其存在权利的镜面。
知更鸟胸臆里盘旋着价值
它随季节迁徙，将所有感受归位，
恰似螃蟹坚守勇气
执着于以视物、行动与执着相连的方式
让世人知晓其存在。

Justice wears itself on a TIGER's stripes
as he walks in the heat of jungle
to discern the balance of nature's subjects.
It works itself into a WOODPECKER's goals
as it knocks on trees to locate food or make a home.
It runs wild through an OCTUPUS' ink
if you dare to wrangle with the trust
of the innocent and the unseen.

न्याय खुद को एक बाघ की धारियों पर धारण करता है जब वह जंगल की गर्मी में चलता है प्रकृति के प्राणियों के संतुलन को परखने के लिए। यह खुद को एक कठफोड़वा के लक्ष्यों में समाहित कर लेता है जब वह भोजन खोजने या घर बनाने के लिए पेड़ों पर चोंच मारता है। यह एक ऑक्टोपस की स्याही में उग्रता से दौड़ता है यदि आप निर्दोष और अदृश्य के विश्वास के साथ संघर्ष करने की हिम्मत करते हैं।

正义披挂在虎纹之上
当它穿行丛林的灼热
辨明自然臣民的平衡。
它融入啄木鸟的目标
当它叩击树干寻觅食物筑巢。
它在章鱼墨汁里奔涌
若你敢质疑那无辜与未见之物的信任。

∞

Hope is the hopping of a RABBIT
after storms were sent to chase her down.
It sings in the breathing of a SWALLOW
that knows every flight could be its last,
and it glides and expands with a SEAHORSE
that glows with its own light in the dark.

आशा एक खरगोश की उछल-कूद है, जब उसे पकड़ने के लिए तूफ़ान भेजे गए हों। यह एक गौरैया की साँसों में गूँजती है, जो जानती है कि उसकी हर उड़ान अंतिम हो सकती है, और यह एक समुद्री घोड़े के साथ तैरती और फैलती है, जो अँधेरे में अपनी ही रोशनी से चमकता है।

∞

希望是野兔的蹦跳
纵使暴风雨追逐不休
它在燕子的呼吸里歌唱
明知每次翱翔都可能是终点
它随海马翱翔舒展
在黑暗中绽放自身光芒

Truth lies in a WOLF that tells no lies
but guards, guides and governs his pack.
It stretches into the shades of a HAWK
who dances in the skies but dives to arrive.
It lives in the teeth of a SHARK
that makes no sound when it appears
like it always had been there all along.

सत्य एक भेड़िये में निहित है जो झूठ नहीं बोलता बल्कि अपनी झुंड की रक्षा करता है, उसका मार्गदर्शन करता है और उसे नियंत्रित करता है। यह एक बाज़ की परछाइयों में फैलता है जो आसमान में नाचता है पर पहुंचने के लिए गोता लगाता है। यह एक शार्क के दाँतों में बसता है जो प्रकट होने पर कोई आवाज़ नहीं करता जैसे कि वह हमेशा से वहीं मौजूद था।

真理栖身于永不撒谎的狼
它守护、引领并统御着狼群
它延伸至猎鹰的阴影
翱翔天际却俯冲而至
它存活于鲨鱼的利齿
悄然现身毫无声息
仿佛自古便在此守候

Peace wallows in a PANDA's attitude
because he knows the wisdom of ignoring criticism
that does not define his worth when he already
knows his roots, colour and nationality.
It gracefully hums in the elegant sailing
of a SWAN on a lake and in the slow steps
of TURTLE that walks towards the ocean
like it has all the time in the world.

शांति एक पांडा के स्वभाव में निहित है क्योंकि वह आलोचना को अनदेखा करने की बुद्धिमानी जानता है जो उसकी कीमत नहीं बताती जब वह पहले से ही अपनी जड़ें, रंग और राष्ट्रीयता जानता है। यह एक झील पर हंस की सुरुचिपूर्ण नौकायन में और समुद्र की ओर चलती कछुए की धीमी चाल में सुंदरता से गुनगुनाती है जैसे उसके पास दुनिया का सारा समय हो।

∞

和平沉醉于熊猫的姿态
因它懂得无视诋毁的智慧
当它已然明晰自身根源、毛色与国籍
那些诋毁便无法定义其价值。
它在天鹅优雅的湖面航行中轻吟
也在乌龟缓步向海洋行进时低语
仿佛拥有世间所有时光。

Space For You

∞

High Standards For You

Space For You

Reena Doss

Space For You

∞

High Standards For You

Space For You

Reena Doss

Acknowledgements

I am grateful

Love produces empathy. Empathy ignites kindness. Kindness inspires respect. Respect honours Humanity. Humanity illuminates faith. Faith teaches patience. Patience strengthens integrity. Integrity reveals values. Values discern justice. Justice affirms hope. Hope births peace. Peace cherishes love.

Gratitude for *Ink Gladiators Press' team—Leonie Belle Hawk, Justin Adam Wolf,* and *Aelius Arche*—for helping me with layout, formatting, design, editing, and proofing. This is my cycle of learning an internal path towards transformation. It may occur in different ways for others, but each of these intangible attributes are earned when I applied myself to the hard lessons, allowed myself to be moulded by the Weaver, and chose His voice instead of the seas of noise. These attributes are not easily imitated, nor can it be unlearned once you have it.

All are seeds and they stem from love. All are given to us when we are born. All become part of the self if we choose to act on them rather than our original nature. When they are seeds at origin, they will keep growing if you let them. If they are plants, they must be tended to. And if they produce flowers, they will automatically reflect the honour of the one who taught you well.

This is why I always thank the Weaver for the way he holds me carefully, restores my soul with laughter, and brings peace after others' storms, or their behaviour might try to uproot what he has given me. Not every attribute is perfect, nor will it ever be a completely grown tree. That is because the unconditional depths of these are borrowed light from the Weaver. They cannot exist without Him. Because He is the Light that I lean on.

May the quill of hope find you in the dark,

Reena Doss

I'll find you in the dark...

Born in Calcutta with roots drawn from Chennai and Pondicherry, Reena Doss has lived most of her life in the south of India—Bangalore. Though she prefers traveling to far-off places inside her head, she sometimes ventures into the world that others call real.

Reena Doss considers writing to be her first voice of expression, followed closely by art, and creativity. Through the encouraging platform provided by the Instagram community, she reclaimed her lost voices, evolved a few others and discovered new ones along the way.

This has redeemed her trust that consistent Hope, Faith and Love in what is true ignites what is impossible to occur. Her adoration for her beloved Weaver, the Celestial Sky, Nature and her fellow Earthians has given her immeasurable courage to endure every season with a resilience born from battles overcome.

You can try and catch her but it may not always be possible as she is generally off on adventures flying on phoenix wings, swimming into the deep with mermaids and chasing fiery dragons down for stories.

To those who remain true to themselves,
to those who create magic wherever they go,
and for those who sit beside the hurt
when everyone else leaves,
Art will always immortalize you.

Please scan the QR code to follow her on
Instagram @reenadossauthor
www.reenadoss.com

This little book is called a *Lantern* because love is light in disguise. It can only be found when you are buried in the dark, when the seeds die, and you choose to bravely grow and become worthy of your given name—a polished gem, a diamond that cannot help but shine. Lanterns are meant for those who need hope while they are being:

- ♥ Condemned unjustly by those who see a version they want
- ♥ Gossiped about when they are not present to defend themselves
- ♥ Taken advantage of when they were beaten down by life, by those who should have stood by them
- ♥ Judged, neglected, and persecuted while they are struggling
- ♥ Abandoned by those who willingly chose to see them as toxic because it suited their narrative
- ♥ Manipulated by those who bore false witness against them to take what wasn't theirs
- ♥ Gaslit, broken, and their truth erased while they were at their most vulnerable
- ♥ Hated, harassed, and purposefully pressured into giving up on who they are because of others' jealousy
- ♥ Trying to process trauma to speak in a language that isn't being heard
- ♥ Eagerly isolated by loved ones on the advice of others who can't understand them any more
- ♥ Neglected by those whose promises dimmed when things got difficult
- ♥ Treated as outcasts by those who expect their will to be done
- ♥ Mocked for what they do just because it is different and does not fit into any box

Promoting hope and unwrapping the stigma of mental health

For any inquiries, please email us at contact@inkgladiatorspress.com.
Please scan the QR Code below if you would like to follow us
on Instagram @inkgladiatorspress.

Ink Gladiators Press®

Publishing and promoting warriors on life's battlefield

9 789349 117426

Printed at Repro India Ltd.